S
A
N

D
I
E
G
O

MICHAEL E. GOODMAN

THE HISTORY OF THE

# PADRES

CREATIVE EDUCATION

Published by Creative Education
123 South Broad Street, Mankato, Minnesota 56001
Creative Education is an imprint of The Creative Company

Designed by Rita Marshall
Editorial assistance by Tracey Cramer & John Nichols

Photos by: Allsport Photography, Anthony Neste, Associated Press/Wide
World Photos, Focus on Sports, Fotosport, SportsChrome.

**Library of Congress Cataloging-in-Publication Data**

Goodman, Michael E.
The History of the San Diego Padres / by Michael E. Goodman.
p. cm. — (Baseball)
Summary: A team history of the San Diego Padres, a minor league franchise
for many years, but a major league member since 1969.
ISBN: 0-88682-923-2

1. San Diego Padres (Baseball team)—History—Juvenile literature.
[1. San Diego Padres (Baseball team)—History.  2. Baseball—History.]
I. Title.  II. Series: Baseball (Mankato, Minn.)

GV875.S33G66   1999
796.357'64'09794985—dc21                                    97-6340

First edition

9  8  7  6  5  4  3  2  1

In 1542, a Spanish explorer named Cabrillo landed his ship along the Pacific Coast just north of where Mexico and the United States meet today. After absorbing the natural beauty of the area, the awestruck explorer was certain he had discovered an island paradise, known in Spanish legend as California. Over the next few years, a settlement was established in the area. The Spanish settlers named it San Diego, after their patron saint. More than 450 years later, San Diego, California, still strikes its visitors as a paradise.

The city has now blossomed into an urban area of more than one million people. It features some of the country's

*A member of the first Padres team, Nate Colbert.*

*Pitcher Dick Selma led the young Padres to their first win by defeating Houston 2–1.*

finest attractions—the spacious sun-soaked harbor, the popular theme park SeaWorld, and some of the most beautiful stretches of beachfront property on the globe. Because of its appeal, some people who visit or live in the city for a short time decide to settle there forever.

Just as the city of San Diego has progressed over the years, so has the community's baseball team. For many years, the San Diego Padres were a minor-league franchise. Then, in 1969, the National League decided to add two new teams. The cities of Montreal and San Diego were chosen as expansion sites.

The Padres have experienced many more losing seasons than winning ones, but things are changing, and the Padres—like the city of San Diego itself—are definitely on the rise. With star players like Tony Gwynn, Ken Caminiti, and Steve Finley, Padres fans believe their team will soon bring the city its first world championship.

## STARTING AT THE BOTTOM

During San Diego's first few years in the National League, Padres fans didn't dare dream of a championship; they just hoped for a winning streak. Even so, their wishes weren't fulfilled very often. The Padres finished dead last in the National League West Division their first six seasons.

Like most expansion clubs, the Padres were built with castoffs from other teams and untried youngsters. The Opening Day lineup in 1969 featured such "stars" as Ollie Brown, Chris Cannizzaro, Rafael Robles, and Ed Spiezio. All of them were drafted from the bottom of the other teams' rosters.

*Dominating closer Trevor Hoffman.*

*Outfielder Cito Gaston earned a spot on the NL All-Star team and Padres MVP honors.*

The Opening Day pitcher was Dick Selma, who had started just five games in the previous four seasons when he played for the New York Mets. Amazingly, Selma and his teammates won that first game—but not many afterward.

Two players picked up in the 1969 expansion draft, however, turned out to be diamonds in the rough and team leaders during the early 1970s. They were Clarence "Cito" Gaston, a smooth-swinging outfielder, and Nate Colbert, a powerful and sure-handed first baseman.

In 1970 Gaston batted .318, a team record for many years. Unfortunately, he never came close to matching his 1970 totals again and was traded after 1974. Colbert also had only a few fine seasons, but he was responsible for one of the greatest thrills in Padres history and one of the finest offensive performances ever.

The date was August 1, 1972. The Padres were facing off in a doubleheader against the Braves in Atlanta. In the first game, Colbert slammed two home runs and two singles, driving in five runs. He then topped those totals in the second game with three more homers, including a grand slam, and eight RBIs. At the end of his incredible day, Colbert had collected five homers, 22 total bases, and 13 RBIs—major league records for a doubleheader.

As Colbert circled the bases after his fifth home run of the day, umpire Bruce Froemming told him, "I don't believe this." Colbert replied, "I don't either. This is unreal."

For five seasons—from 1969 to 1973—Colbert was one of the National League's top sluggers, averaging more than 30 home runs a year. Then pitchers began feeding him a steady diet of curveballs that he had trouble hitting, and Colbert soon retired from the game.

Despite Gaston's and Colbert's heroics, the Padres kept losing, and San Diego fans stopped coming out to the ballpark to watch them play. Things got so bad that team owner C. Arnholt Smith decided to move the team across the country to Washington, D.C., just before the 1974 season. New uniforms were manufactured, and the club's files and equipment were all packed for the move. Then Ray Kroc, the owner of the McDonald's restaurant chain, stepped in. He offered to buy the club from Smith and keep it in San Diego. Smith accepted the offer, and the San Diego Padres had a new lease on life.

**1 9 7 3**

*The dependable Bill Greif led San Diego in ERA, innings pitched, complete games, and shutouts.*

## DEVELOPING A WINNING ATTITUDE

R ay Kroc not only rescued the Padres' franchise in 1974, he also helped the club develop a winning attitude. The team had finished last for five straight seasons, and losing had become a habit. Kroc knew the team already had several young potential stars, including left-handed pitcher Randy Jones and outfielder Dave Winfield, a player so athletically gifted that he was drafted by four teams in three different professional sports after his standout career at the University of Minnesota. Kroc decided that what the Padres needed was a new manager, as well as some veteran players who knew what winning was like.

First, Kroc hired John McNamara as his manager. McNamara was an excellent teacher and leader. "He was a quiet,

*Bruce Hurst was a successful lefty.*

*Outfielder Dave Winfield.*  11

**1  9  7  4**

*In his first year in a Padres uniform, Willie McCovey led the club in homers with 22.*

thoughtful man you could really talk to," Winfield said. "He'd point out any problems with your play, suggest things you might work on. But mostly he'd emphasize what you were doing right."

Next, Kroc made a trade with the San Francisco Giants for future Hall-of-Famer Willie McCovey. Although McCovey was near the end of his great career, he was just what the Padres' youngsters needed. "He was dignified, quiet, easygoing—a truly generous human being. I'm not sure why, but when he came to San Diego in 1974, he took me under his wing," Winfield remarked.

One day, the aging superstar taught his young friend a valuable lesson. "He was at bat, and I was on deck," Winfield remembered. "The other team's outfielders were playing him where they almost always did—deep. So Willie took a monster cut and missed on the first pitch to make sure they'd stay there. Then on the next pitch, he laid down a perfect bunt, just to get himself on base. 'I did it so you could knock me in,' he told me later. I did just that, and I learned as much about strategy in that moment as I had in the 21 years preceding it."

Even with McCovey and Winfield, the Padres finished last again in 1974. But Ray Kroc wasn't discouraged. He didn't really expect his team to become a championship contender overnight. His plan called for gradual improvement, and it seemed to work.

The next year, the Padres climbed out of the basement for the first time, finishing in fourth place. During that season, McCovey smacked 23 homers and Winfield hit 15. Together they drove in more than 150 runs. Also, Randy Jones discovered a new way to throw his curveball that caused it to break sharply and made him almost unhittable. Jones, who had lost 22 games in 1974, became a 20-game winner in 1975. The next year he was even better, winning 22 games, and he was given the Cy Young Award as the National League's best pitcher.

After the 1976 season, Jones revealed the secret behind his new award-winning delivery: "I always try to release the ball over a bent front leg. On every delivery, I go through certain checkpoints. I have to let the ball go in front of me— not even with my head, but in front of my body. I also make sure I drop down on my back leg, the left leg that's on the mound, so that I get a good push off the mound."

For the first time in Padres history, the team was getting good pitching and consistent hitting. Things were certainly changing for the better in San Diego. However, the club still had not recorded a winning season. In 1978, the franchise's 10th year in the league, that would change too.

In 1977 and 1978, Kroc brought in two more veteran "winners"—first, ace relief pitcher Rollie Fingers, and later, former Cy Young Award recipient Gaylord Perry. The Padres also promoted a young fielding wizard named Ozzie Smith from their minor-league system to take over at shortstop. The newcomers added an important spark to the team. With Winfield hitting more than .300 for the first time in his career and knocking in nearly 100 runs, Perry winning 21 games, and Fingers recording a league-leading 37 saves, the Padres finished the 1978 season with an 84–78 record. San Diego might not have been playoff-bound yet, but it was a winner at last.

1 9 7 8

*For the second consecutive season, relief pitcher Rollie Fingers was the NL's Fireman of the Year.*

*In his first season with the Padres, shortstop Garry Templeton led the team in runs scored with 76.*

For the next few years, the Padres' fortunes went up and down. The team's big problems were inconsistency and player turnover. The strain of the 315 innings Jones pitched in 1976 left him with a tired arm and control problems. He was traded to the New York Mets after the 1980 season. Fingers and Perry were also traded for younger players. Smith continued to shine in the field, but his undeveloped offensive skills led the Padres to swap him to St. Louis for Garry Templeton. Then Winfield, who had become the team's main star, demanded more money when his contract came up after the 1980 season. San Diego management balked, and Winfield packed his bags and headed east to the New York Yankees.

By the start of the 1982 season, a whole new cast was in place in San Diego. The new players included outfielders Sixto Lezcano and Ruppert Jones, infielders Garry Templeton and Luis Salazar, catcher Terry Kennedy, and pitchers Tim Lollar, Andy Hawkins, and Eric Show. There was also a new manager, Dick Williams, who had previously skippered the Boston Red Sox to an American League pennant, the Oakland A's to two world championships, and the Montreal Expos to an NL East Division title.

Williams was a no-nonsense manager who demanded the very best from his players. "We'll start developing a winning habit the first day of spring training," proclaimed the new manager. Under Williams's direction, the players came roaring out of spring training and set a team record with an 11-game winning streak in April. By mid-July, they were 14

*Cy Young Award winner Gaylord Perry.*

games over .500 (50–36) and just two games behind the first-place Atlanta Braves.

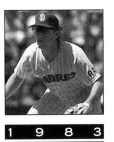

But the success would not continue. The Padres faltered in the last two months of the season, finishing in fourth place in the division with an even 81–81 record. Yet optimism remained. It was only the second time in team history that the Padres had won as many games as they had lost. San Diego fans were encouraged. Dick Williams had the Padres working well as a team.

*The signing of third baseman Graig Nettles after the season was one of the Padres' best transactions.*

"Dick told us at the beginning that team play was in, and excuses were out," said catcher Terry Kennedy, who led the team in batting (.295), homers (21), and RBIs (97). "He told us that the manager doesn't pick the team—the players do it by their own performance. That left it

*The incomparable Tony Gwynn.*

up to each one of us," he explained. "If you produced, you played. Simple as that."

During the 1982 season, Williams got his players to believe in themselves. But the team still lacked the overall talent to become a consistent winner. Williams and San Diego general manager Jack McKeon decided to undertake a rebuilding process, combining established veterans and hungry young players.

First, McKeon signed former Dodgers great Steve Garvey to play first base in 1983. Garvey solidified the Padres' infield and added another consistent hitter to the lineup. "He gives us the right-handed power we've needed," said Williams.

Before the 1984 season, the team acquired two stars from the Yankee championship teams of the late 1970s—fireballing relief pitcher Rich "Goose" Gossage and slugging third baseman Graig Nettles. Opposing batters feared Gossage's blazing fastballs. "Getting him gives us instant credibility," Williams announced. "He's going to take a lot of pressure off our young pitching staff. They know if they get in trouble, Goose is out there in the bullpen to bail them out."

Nettles, at age 40, remained one of the most explosive hitters and one of the steadiest third basemen in the majors. The six-time All-Star also brought a wealth of championship experience and leadership to the team. "Graig's a winner, and we need him to get us over the hump," Williams said.

Having taken care of the infield and bullpen with veterans, McKeon then rebuilt the Padres' outfield with three kids—Carmelo Martinez, Kevin McReynolds, and Tony Gwynn.

With all of the pieces in place, the Padres were set to take on the rest of the National League in 1984. "We've got things

**1 9 8 4**

*The Padres dedicated their finest season to owner Ray Kroc, who died in January.*

*Slugger Kevin McReynolds (pages 18–19).*    17

going for us now," Williams told sportswriters before the season began. "We're ready."

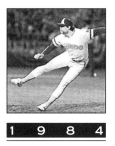

**1 9 8 4**

*Relief pitcher Rich Gossage joined teammates Steve Garvey and Tony Gwynn on the NL All-Star squad.*

## PENNANT CONTENDER MAKES ITS MOVE

**S**an Diego fans were also ready. A near-record crowd of 44,553 people jammed Jack Murphy Stadium on Opening Day in 1984 to watch the Padres drum the Pittsburgh Pirates, 5–1. The victory was a sign of good things to come.

The Padres' early success continued as they pulled away from the pack. By midsummer, the club was nine games in front of the second-place Houston Astros and well on their way to their first division title.

The San Diego fans were jubilant. There was, however, a sad note. Ray Kroc, the man most responsible for keeping the Padres in San Diego and building the franchise, never got to see his team win its first title. Early in 1984, Kroc had died. Fittingly, the team dedicated its finest season to him.

The biggest and most pleasant surprise of the year was the hitting of right fielder Tony Gwynn. In his first full major-league season, he won the league batting title with a .351 average, smacked 213 hits, stole 33 bases, and won a starting spot on the NL All-Star team.

"Tony is in a class all by himself," remarked his batting coach, Deacon Jones. "He knows the strike zone, makes good contact, hits to all fields, and has the speed to beat out infield hits. He likes to hit, and he believes in himself. He takes an extra five minutes of batting practice every day and studies videotapes to detect any flaws."

"I just go up there, see the ball, and swing," said Gwynn modestly. "I guess a lot of it is God-given ability. I just want to sit back on the ball and put it in play."

Padres fans got their first long look at the almost-certain future Hall of Famer in 1984, and his performance during the NL Championship Series turned even more heads.

The Padres faced the favored Chicago Cubs, and in the first two games in Chicago, the Cubs dominated, winning both contests by a combined score of 17–1. When the series turned to Jack Murphy Stadium, the San Diego fans poured through the turnstiles and breathed some much-needed new life back into their shaken club. "We were real nervous and tight during the games in Chicago," explained Gwynn. "A lot of us had never been in a game that big. It wasn't until we got back to San Diego in front of our fans that we finally relaxed."

The relaxed Padres bashed the Cubs 7–1 in game three behind the pitching of Ed Whitson and Goose Gossage and the slugging of Kevin McReynolds. In game four, San Diego jumped out to an early lead, then fell into a tie heading into the bottom of the ninth—but not for long. Steve Garvey ended things by smacking a two-run homer to give the Padres the victory. The pennant came down to one game.

In the final contest, the Cubs staked their pitching ace Rick Sutcliffe to a 3–0 lead after five innings. The Padres scratched back for two runs in the sixth and tied the game with one out in the seventh. Then, with runners on first and third, Gwynn stepped up. With a smooth swing of his bat, he smashed a wicked line-drive double just past the outstretched glove of Cubs star second baseman Ryne Sandberg

*Tony Gwynn led the San Diego club in batting average (.317), runs (90), and hits (197).*

*NL Rookie of the Year Benito Santiago.*

for the go-ahead run. Garvey followed with a single for two more runs, building a 6–3 lead. "That was a big moment for me," smiled Gwynn. "Every kid dreams about getting the big hit when the game's on the line. I was just lucky enough to live it."

After that, it was up to the veteran closer Goose Gossage. The big right-hander slammed the door on the Cubs in the last two innings to preserve the win and send the Padres to their first World Series. Gwynn, who had tattooed Chicago pitching to the tune of a .368 average, was ecstatic. "I wish this moment could last forever. The people of San Diego have been waiting, and it feels so good to give them something to be proud of."

*With a 3.07 ERA, Dave Dravecky led the San Diego club for the second year in a row.*

Unfortunately for San Diego fans, the Padres were burned out after the grueling series with the Cubs and were no match for the powerful American League champion Detroit Tigers. After the teams split the first two games in San Diego, the Tigers won three straight in Detroit to capture the world championship. Despite the loss, more than 40,000 grateful Padres followers attended a "victory" celebration at Jack Murphy Stadium when the Padres returned home.

## CONTINUING UPS AND DOWNS

The Padres and their fans were on top of the world after the 1984 season. They expected big things in 1985, but the club was not able to fulfill its promise. First, the team's excellent lead-off hitter, Alan Wiggins, was suspended from baseball because of drug problems. "Losing Alan shook our offense," manager Dick Williams said.

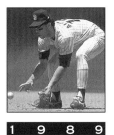

*Slick-fielding second baseman Roberto Alomar tied for the team lead in doubles and runs scored.*

Wiggins' suspension and the declining production of aging veterans Nettles, Garvey, and Gossage caused the favored Padres to fall to third place in the NL West in 1985.

Then, internal battling within the Padres' management led Williams to resign in 1986, and bickering between players and management destroyed the last bits of the unity forged in 1984. By the end of the 1987 season, the team had fallen to last place again.

General manager Jack McKeon decided to find a new manager to help turn things around. Believing in the old saying, "If you want things done right, do it yourself," McKeon appointed himself as manager. Then he put on his general manager's hat and spent the rest of the 1980s wheeling and dealing to acquire the right players to put the Padres on top again.

He already had baseball's best hitter, Tony Gwynn, on his squad. He also had the 1987 Rookie of the Year, catcher Benito Santiago, and soon the general manager brought up some excellent youngsters from the minor-league system. These players included infielders Roberto Alomar and Bip Roberts, both of whom had the potential to be .300 hitters and to steal 30 to 40 bases a year. With Gwynn, Santiago, Alomar, and Roberts, McKeon had built a strong young nucleus, but he wasn't done yet. He needed to add pitching and power to the mix as well. In a wild flurry of trading and signing, he acquired hurlers Bruce Hurst, Ed Whitson, Mark Grant, and Craig Lefferts, as well as sluggers Jack Clark, Joe Carter, and Mike Pagliarulo.

After the dust settled, McKeon was certain that he had molded a National League championship team for the

1990s. Unfortunately, the team didn't start the new decade like champions. The Padres' fearsome lineup scored lots of runs in the early '90s, but San Diego pitchers gave up just as many. The team won and lost games in streaks; its inconsistent performances disappointed San Diego fans.

Still, Jack Murphy Stadium saw its share of excitement. In 1991, Gwynn joined forces with talented teammate Fred McGriff to form a dynamic offensive duo. Gwynn hit .317, setting the table for first baseman McGriff, who belted 31 homers and drove in 106 runs.

1 9 9 1

*Fred McGriff became the fourth player in NL history to blast grand slams in consecutive games.*

In 1992, the duo became a trio when powerful third baseman Gary Sheffield came over in a trade with the Milwaukee Brewers. Putting Sheffield's lightning-quick bat behind Gwynn and McGriff spelled disaster for National League pitchers. Gwynn hit .317 again, McGriff clubbed 35 homers with 104 RBIs, and Sheffield won the batting title, hitting .330 with a team-record .580 slugging percentage. "They gotta break those guys up," muttered frustrated Pittsburgh Pirates manager Jim Leyland. "They just wore my staff out." The Padres' shaky pitching could not be overcome, however. Despite the heroics of Gwynn, McGriff, and Sheffield, the team faded late in 1992, finishing 82–80.

The end of the 1992 season also saw the start of what industry observers have labeled the Padres' "fire sale"—a year of utter chaos for the San Diego team. The roster was slashed following heavy budget cutbacks.

Despite Sheffield's performance, he was traded to the Florida Marlins. McGriff was traded to the Atlanta Braves for three minor-leaguers. Pitcher Craig Lefferts was traded to Baltimore, and pitchers Greg Harris and Bruce Hurst were

*1996 National League MVP Ken Caminiti (pages 26–27).*

also dumped. Randy Myers (38 saves in '92) and All-Star catcher Benito Santiago left as free agents. The changes crippled the Padres' roster and lowered morale throughout the organization. As a result, San Diego posted a feeble 61–101 record in 1993.

In the wake of these catastrophic changes, some observers predicted the purging would ruin the Padres' championship chances for years to come, but new general manager Randy Smith began slowly rebuilding the San Diego team. In December of 1994, he made a blockbuster trade with the Houston Astros that involved 12 players. The trade was the fourth-largest in baseball this century, and for the Padres it was the start of better days.

**1 9 9 3**

*Gary Sheffield led the Padres in runs (87) and hits (184), and led the league with a .330 batting average.*

### PADRES LOOK TO A CHAMPIONSHIP FUTURE

When Randy Smith pulled the trigger on what would soon be known in San Diego as "The Trade," many baseball observers saw the move as a desperate gamble. "The Padres' free-fall continues," wrote one newspaper. But Smith had a hunch about two of his new players, and luckily for San Diego fans, he was right. "I always thought Ken Caminiti and Steve Finley were two of the toughest competitors we played year in and year out," explained Randy Smith. "I thought if we could add their toughness, it would help, but I had no idea it would work out like it did."

In 1995 and 1996, Caminiti and Finley not only added toughness to the Padres, but both veterans contributed back-to-back career seasons.

The fleet Finley has always been one of baseball's finest

center fielders, but with his slender build, (6-foot-2 and 180 pounds), he had never hit for much power. "I've never been a power guy, not with this body," laughed Finley. "But I've learned to drive it some the last couple years." Finley belted 10 homers in '95, and then an amazing 30 in 1996, while driving in 95 runs and winning the second of two straight Gold Glove awards for his excellence in the field.

The switch-hitting Caminiti lends a fiery attitude, along with his booming bat and sure glove. "Ken is just so intense," said Padres manager Bruce Bochy. "It's hard to explain, because I've never met anybody like him before."

Caminiti's legendary toughness came into play when the Padres hosted the Mets in a 1996 game held in Monterrey, Mexico. Scheduling problems had forced the game to be moved south of the border, and several players from both teams had become ill. Suffering from food poisoning and dehydration, he lay on the clubhouse floor taking intravenous fluids. Barely able to walk, Caminiti still insisted on playing. After wobbling onto the field and surviving the top of the first inning at third base, Caminiti made his way back to the dugout, downed a candy bar, and then proceeded to belt the first of two home runs to spark the Padres to an 8–0 win. "That was the most amazing thing I've ever seen," said teammate Tony Gwynn.

Caminiti hit 40 homers and drove in 130 runs for the Padres in 1996, and he was a unanimous selection as the National League MVP. He also won his second consecutive Gold Glove award for his play at third base. Spurred by the efforts of their two new stars, the Padres raced to the top of the National League West once again in 1996, finishing

**1 9 9 8**

*Wally Joyner, who hit a career-high .327 the previous season, was expected to lead the club.*

*Young pitching ace, Joey Hamilton.*

*Versatile outfielder Steve Finley.*     31

91–71. In the postseason, the Padres drew the St. Louis Cardinals. Although they battled fiercely, San Diego was swept in three straight games.

With Finley and Caminiti just hitting their prime and Gwynn aging like fine wine, the Padres appear set to be among the league's elite for the foreseeable future. Much of their fate rests on young pitchers like Joey Hamilton, Andy Ashby and star closer Trevor Hoffman. "We've got the bats," said Gwynn, "We just need our young pitchers to keep improving, and we'll have a championship future."

For Padres fans, the improvement has already been impressive, as their team, left for dead in 1993, now challenges for the ultimate prize—a World Series title.